TRAVERSE
THEATRE

Traverse Theatre Company
The Ballad of Crazy Paola
by Arne Sierens
in a version by Stephen Greenhorn

cast in order of appearance

Paola Kathryn Howden
Raymond Billy Boyd

director Philip Howard
designer Mark Leese
lighting designer Maria Bechaalani
composer Paddy Cunneen
script associate Katherine Mendelsohn
voice coach Ros Steen
assistant director Helen-Marie O'Malley
literal translator Paul Gilling
stage manager Gavin Harding
deputy stage manager Christine Knibbs
assistant stage manager Kirsty Paton
wardrobe supervisor Lynn Ferguson
wardrobe assistant Stephanie Thorburn

**First performed at the Traverse Theatre
Friday 5 October 2001**

TRAVERSE THEATRE
powerhouse of new writing DAILY TELEGRAPH

Artistic Director Philip Howard

The Traverse is Scotland's new writing theatre. Founded in 1963 by a group of maverick artists and enthusiasts, it began as an imaginative attempt to capture the spirit of adventure and experimentation of the Edinburgh Festival all year round. Throughout the decades, the Traverse has evolved and grown in artistic output and ambition. It has refined its mission by strengthening its commitment to producing new plays by Scottish and international playwrights and actively nurturing them throughout their careers. Traverse productions have been seen worldwide and tour regularly throughout the UK and overseas.

The Traverse has produced over 600 new plays in its lifetime and, through a spirit of innovation and risk-taking, has launched the careers of many of the country's best known writers. From, among others, Stanley Eveling in the 1960s, John Byrne in the 1970s, Liz Lochhead in the 1980s, David Greig in the 1990s to Gregory Burke in the 2000s, the Traverse is unique in Scotland in its dedication to new writing. It fulfils the crucial role of providing the infrastructure, professional support and expertise to ensure the development of a dynamic theatre culture for Scotland.

The Traverse's activities encompass every aspect of playwriting and production, providing and facilitating play reading panels, script development workshops, rehearsed readings, public playwriting workshops, writers groups, a public playwrights' platform The Monday Lizard, discussions and special events. The Traverse's work with young people is of supreme importance and takes the form of encouraging playwriting through its flagship education project, Class Act, as well as the Traverse Young Writers Group.

Edinburgh's Traverse Theatre is a mini-festival in itself
THE TIMES

From its conception in the 1960s, the Traverse has remained a pivotal venue during the Edinburgh Festival. It receives enormous critical and audience acclaim for its programming, as well as regularly winning awards. The year 2001 was no different with the Traverse being awarded 2 Scotsman Fringe Firsts and two Herald Angels for its own productions *Gagarin Way* and *Wiping My Mother's Arse* and a Herald Archangel for overall artistic excellence. *Gagarin Way* also recieved a First of the Firsts award from The Scotsman.

For further information on the Traverse Theatre's activities and history, an online resource is available at www.virtualtraverse.com. To find out about ways to support the Traverse, please contact Jayne Gross, Development Manager on 0131 228 3223.

The Ballad of Crazy Paola was commissioned under the Traverse Theatre's Playwrights in Partnership Scheme in association with the Paul Hamlyn Foundation, matching Scottish playwrights with their international counterparts.

The Traverse would also like to thank the Vlaams Institute in Belgium for their support with this project.

Traverse Theatre Company small scale tour and writers' project

The Traverse Theatre Company has been touring to small scale venues throughout the Highlands and Islands since 1993 with new plays and a fully integrated Writers' Project. It has produced plays of an excellent quality from both established writers (Iain Crichton Smith in 1997) and emerging writers (Henry Adam in 2000). We are committed to broadening the geographical spread of our tours and last year took in venues in the North East and the Borders. 2001 sees us returning to many of our regular venues as well as venturing to Glasgow and West Lothian.

Writers' Project 2001

How can you re-imagine a play from a different language when you don't even speak it?!

This year's Writers Project is led by Philip Howard, Artistic Director of the Traverse and director of *The Ballad of Crazy Paola*, and Helen-Marie O'Malley, Assistant Director. It focuses on the fascinating and thorny issue of translation and how to set about transferring plays from one culture to another.

No previous experience of playwriting required, but workshops will include practical writing exercises. Participants must have a ticket for the play.

Writers workshops are available in Ballachulish, Inverness, Ardross, Orkney, Findhorn and Ullapool. Please contact Catherine MacNeil on 0131 228 3223 for full details or email catherine@traverse.co.uk.

For customers in Yetholm, there is a FREE taster workshop for the Traverse Borders Writers Group on Sat 20 Oct at the St Andrew's Arts Centre, Galashiels. To participate, please contact Pauline Diamond on 0131 228 3223.

BIOGRAPHIES

ARNE SIERENS
Studied stage direction at the HRITCS in Brussels. He began his directing career working with existing repertoire, classical and modern before writing and directing his own plays. In 1981 he set up the theatre company Sluipende Armoede (Sneaking Poverty) which provided the framework for several of his plays. He now works freelance as a playwright and director. He recently completed a successful trilogy of plays in collaboration with the choreographer Alain Platel which have toured extensively around the world: MOEDER EN KIND, BERNADTJE and ALLEMAAL INDIAN. His latest production NOT ALL MORROCCANS ARE THEIVES is currently touring Europe.

STEPHEN GREENHORN
For the Traverse: PASSING PLACES. Recent work for theatre includes: KING MATT (TAG Theatre Company); ELECTION, DISSENT, THE SALT WOUND (7:84 Theatre Company); SLEEP-ING AROUND (Paines Plough); THE BIRDS (The Gate). Stephen has also written drama for TV, radio and film, including GLAS-GOW KISS (BBC). He is currently working on a series for BBC TV and the film of PASSING PLACES for BBC Films.

Maria Bechaalani (lighting designer): Trained at the Bristol Old Vic Theatre School. For the Traverse: HIGHLAND SHORTS. Maria has worked with several venues and companies as an electrician including: The Traverse Theatre, Theatre Archipelago, The Byre, St Andrews, Perth Theatre and Birmingham Rep. She has also worked as a Lighting Designer for companies including: The Byre, Birmingham Rep and Lung Ha's.

Billy Boyd (Raymond): Trained RSAMD. For the Traverse: THE SPECULATOR (a co-production with Edinburgh International Festival), KILL THE OLD TORTURE THEIR YOUNG, THE CHIC NERDS, WIDOWS. Other theatre work includes: AN EXPERIENCED WOMAN GIVES ADVICE, BRITANNIA RULES, HANSEL AND GRETEL, MUCH ADO ABOUT NOTHING, SLEEPING BEAUTY, THE MERCHANT OF VENICE, MERLIN THE MAGNIFICENT (Royal Lyceum); THERESE RAQUIN (Communicado/Royal Lyceum); CALEDONIA DREAMING (7:84); THE PLAZA (Tron Showcase); TRAINSPOTTING (National tour); SLEEPING BEAUTY (Kings Glasgow); MUCH ADO ABOUT NOTHING (Original Shakespeare Co); THE SLAB BOYS, THE SECRET DIARY OF ADRIAN MOLE (Byre). Television work includes: TAGGART (STV); COMING SOON, CHAPTER & VERSE (Channel 4). Film productions include: LORD OF THE RINGS TRILOGY (New Line Cinema); JULIE & THE CADILLACS (ITV); URBAN GHOST STORY (Living Spirit). Radio work includes: HAND IN GLOVE, TAM O'SHANTER, 'P' DIVISION CODE 41, BULLSEYE BABES (BBC).

Paddy Cunneen (composer): For the Traverse: WIPING MY MOTHER'S ARSE. Paddy has worked extensively as a composer and music director for theatres throughout the UK and Ireland. His work runs to over 100 productions for the RNT, RSC, Cheek By Jowl, Donmar Warehouse, Abbey, Gate and Druid Theatres, Manchester Royal Exchange, Royal Court, Liverpool Everyman and many others. In addition he composes for BBC Radio Drama, RTE Radio Drama and has a number of TV and film credits. He is a recipient of the Christopher Whelen Award for Music in Theatre.

Philip Howard (director): Philip trained at the Royal Court Theatre, London, on the Regional Theatre Young Director Scheme from 1988-90. He was Associate Director at the Traverse from 1993-96, and has been Artistic Director since 1996. Productions for the Traverse include: WIPING MY MOTHER'S ARSE, THE TRESTLE AT POPE LICK CREEK, SHETLAND SAGA, SOLEMN MASS FOR A FULL MOON IN SUMMER (with Ros Steen), HIGHLAND SHORTS, THE SPECULATOR, HERITAGE (1998 & 2001), KILL THE OLD TORTURE THEIR YOUNG, THE CHIC NERDS, LAZYBED, WORMWOOD, FAITH HEALER, THE ARCHITECT, KNIVES IN HENS (also The Bush Theatre), EUROPE, BROTHERS OF THUNDER and LOOSE ENDS. Philip's other theatre includes HIPPOLYTUS (Arts Theatre Cambridge); ENTERTAINING MR SLOANE (Royal Theatre, Northampton) and SOMETHING ABOUT US (Lyric Hammersmith Studio).

Kathryn Howden (Paola): Trained RSAMD. For the Traverse: ABANDONMENT, PASSING PLACES, BONDAGERS (Traverse & on tour Canada, London, Budapest), THE HOPE SLIDE, BUCHANAN, POOR SUPERMAN (Traverse/Hampstead). Other theatre work includes: THE GOVERNMENT INSPECTOR (Almeida); NEVER BEFORE SEEN, FAMILIAR, EARTHQUAKE WEATHER, VIPER'S OPIUM (Starving Artists); THE MARRIAGE OF FIGARO, CAN'T PAY? WON'T PAY!, FAMILY AFFAIR, A VIEW FROM THE BRIDGE, THE MERCHANT OF VENICE, THE TAMING OF THE SHREW (Royal Lyceum); ROAD, NAE PROBLEM (7:84 Scotland); DANTON'S DEATH (Communicado); JUST FRANK, SHOOTING DUCKS (Theatre Royal, Stratford East); BEAUTY AND THE BEAST, SWING HAMMER SWING (Citizens'); TARTUFFE, LOSING ALEC (Tron); SEX COMEDIES (Old Red Lion). Television work includes: FORGOTTEN, PEAK PRACTICE, MACRAME MAN, ROCKFACE BIG CAT, TAGGART. Tartan Shorts: THE PEN, KARMIC MOTHERS. Film includes: THE PRIEST AND THE PIRATE (V.I.P.). Kathryn is also an experienced radio broadcaster having recorded many plays for BBC Radio Scotland, Radio 3 and Radio Clyde. Writing work has included a commission from the Traverse for SHARP SHORTS.

Mark Leese (designer): For the Traverse: AMONG UNBROKEN HEARTS, SHETLAND SAGA, THE SPECULATOR, KILL THE OLD TORTURE THEIR YOUNG, KNIVES IN HENS, THE CHIC NERDS, GRETA, ANNA WEISS, WIDOWS, FAITH HEALER, THE HOPE SLIDE, BROTHERS OF THUNDER. Other recent work includes: FROGS (Royal National Theatre); THE PLAYBOY OF THE WEST-ERN WORLD, A FAMILY AFFAIR (Dundee Rep); MARTIN YESTER-DAY (Royal Exchange, Manchester); A WEEKEND IN ENGLAND (Gateway, Chester); THE GREEKS (Theatre Babel); PARALLEL LINES (Theatre Cryptic); BORN GUILTY, THE WAR IN HEAVEN, THE GRAPES OF WRATH, THE SALT WOUND, ANTIGONE (7:84); ON GOLDEN POND (Royal Lyceum). Film work includes: MAGDALENE (PFP Films); HOME (CH4, BAFTA winner); HID-DEN, NIGHT SWIMMER, BILLIE AND ZORBA, SPITTING DIS-TANCE, GOLDEN WEDDING, CANDY FLOSS (BBC), GIRL IN THE LAY BY, GOOD DAY FOR THE BAD GUYS, RUBY (STV), CALIFORNIA SUNSHINE, HEART AND SOLE (CH4). Mark is Design Associate at the Traverse.

The Traverse would like to thank everyone who generously donated equipment, services and time to help on *The Ballad of Crazy Paola*.

Sets, props and costumes for *The Ballad of Crazy Paola* created by Traverse Workshops (funded by the National Lottery)

THE SCOTTISH **ARTS** COUNCIL

National Lottery Fund

production & print photography by Kevin Low

SPONSORSHIP

Sponsorship income enables the Traverse to commission and produce new plays and to offer audiences a diverse and exciting programme of events throughout the year.

We would like to thank the following companies for their support throughout the year:

CORPORATE ASSOCIATE SCHEME

Sunday Herald
Scottish Life the PENSION company
United Distillers & Vintners
Laurence Smith & Son Wine Merchants
Willis Corroon Scotland Ltd
Wired Nomad
Alistir Tait FGA - Antiques & Fine Jewellery
Nicholas Groves Raines - Architects
KPMG
Amanda Howard Associates
Alan Thienot Champagne
Bairds Fine and Country Wines
Communicate
The Wellcome Trust

MAJOR SPONSORS

BBC Scotland

The Traverse Trivia Quiz in association with Tennants

with thanks to: Navy Blue Design Consultants & Stewarts, graphic designers and printers for the Traverse
Arts & Business for management and mentoring services
Purchase of the Traverse Box Office, computer network and technical and training equipment has been made possible with money from The Scottish Arts Council National Lottery Fund

The Traverse receives financial assistance for its educational and development work from Calouste Gulbenkian Foundation, John Lewis Partnership, Peggy Ramsay Foundation, The Yapp Charitable Trusts, Binks Trust, The Bulldog Prinsep Theatrical Trust, Esmee Fairbairn Trust, Gannochy Trust, Gordon Fraser Charitable Trust, The Garfield Weston Foundation, JSP Pollitzer Charitable Trust, The Hope Trust, The Steel Trust, Paul Hamlyn Foundation, The Craignish Trust, Lindsay's Charitable Trust, Tay Charitable Trust, Ernest Cook Trust, The Education Institute of Scotland, supporting arts projects produced by and for children.
Charity No. SC002368

TRAVERSE THEATRE - THE COMPANY

THE BALLAD OF CRAZY PAOLA

Characters

PAOLA

RAYMOND

SCENE ONE

PAOLA *stands by the window in her lounge. The doorbell rings. She moves into the hall and calls upstairs.*

PAOLA.
Nick? Stay there. I'll get it.

She opens the door. RAYMOND *enters, his nose covered with a plaster.*

RAYMOND.
Mrs. Prentice?

PAOLA.
Come in.

RAYMOND.
I'm a bit early.

PAOLA.
It's fine. You found us alright then?

RAYMOND.
After a while. But I always try to give myself plenty of time.

They come in.

PAOLA.
My son'll be down in a minute.
Have a seat. Hang on. I'll get rid of these.
Don't mind the mess. It's been one of those weeks.
My cleaning woman's sick and I haven't had a moment to
     myself.

Nick's studying.
That was one of the conditions for doing this.
The drum lessons. He had to dig in with his studies.
Him and homework! Like trying to teach a cat to swim!

He's not really into sport. Just his music.
His room. Posters everywhere. You should see it.
And now he's discovered graffiti.
Scrawling all sorts over the walls.

Who's going to redecorate? I said. You?
I only did upstairs last year.
Completely washable, they told me. Hah!
Well I've washed my hands of it now.
I'm telling you.

He's got another five minutes.

Pause. RAYMOND *laughs.*

RAYMOND.
My nose. It's a bit scary.

PAOLA.
Did you bump into something?

RAYMOND.
An accident. Few weeks ago.
Nothing serious. I never drive very fast.
But… No seat belt!

PAOLA.
I sometimes forget too.

RAYMOND.
Smack. Steering wheel. Broken.
Two more weeks.

PAOLA.
I should be more careful myself.
So.
You said on the phone that Thursdays were good for you.
Or Saturdays. But Saturdays are …

RAYMOND.
No good.

PAOLA.
No.
Their father has them at the weekends. Mondays and
    Tuesdays are no good either.

RAYMOND.
No. Mondays are out for me.

PAOLA.
And Tuesdays.

RAYMOND.
I have to drive my mother round the shops.

PAOLA.
Wednesdays.

RAYMOND.
Yes. Possibly.

PAOLA.
But you'd have to rearrange things.

RAYMOND.
I could do that. If I had to.
If it suited you better.

PAOLA.
No no. Thursdays are fine.

RAYMOND.
You sure? I could make it Wednesday?

PAOLA.
No. Thursdays. That's what we said.
I mean, if that's okay with him.
You two will have to agree.

RAYMOND.
Yes. Fine. Absolutely.

Pause. She sits down with a sigh.

PAOLA.
That's one thing sorted out at least.
My order book at the moment.
God knows how much work I've got to do this week.
It's always the same. Nothing for ages then everything
    happens at once.
I do flowers.

RAYMOND.
    Oh. Right.

PAOLA.
    Dried flowers mainly. I make little bouquets. Design them
        myself. Ikebana.

    A beat.

PAOLA.
    You've never heard of it, have you.

RAYMOND.
    I've heard of it.

PAOLA.
    I can't complain, I suppose. I do well enough out of it.

    Pause.

PAOLA.
    What about you? Do you play in a group?

RAYMOND.
    No. Not at the moment. I'm talking to some people though.
    Yesterday. They phoned to see if I would audition for them.
    For their band.
    I don't think I'm going to.

PAOLA.
    No?

RAYMOND.
    No. They're just a bunch of kids.
    I have played in lots of groups though.

PAOLA.
    Rock?

RAYMOND.
    And reggae. Funk. Salsa. Everything.

    A beat.

PAOLA.
    The drum kit!
    I just remembered. You should take a look at it.

Nick and I have been arguing about it.

We went out and got one last week but he thinks it's too
small. Inadequate, he says.

He reckons it needs wood blocks. A cow bell. More
cymbals. And a set of hanging chimes.

RAYMOND.

Angel dust.

PAOLA.

I said, look, if it turns out you need more bits and pieces
you can always add to it. Later.

Just start at the beginning. Learn to hold the sticks properly!

He's got a bass drum. A snare. A high-hat. Two toms and
two cymbals. That's enough to get him started.

Isn't it?

RAYMOND.

Should be.

PAOLA.

You know what those shop displays are like though.

Unbelievable. They'd take up half the stage on their own!

I said, start with the basics. See if you can keep the beat
first.

She looks at her watch.

PAOLA.

Let's go and see.

I'd better warn you. He can be an awkward customer when
he wants to be, my son. Thinks he can do everything
at once. You'll have to watch that. He's pretty full of
himself is Nick.

They head toward the back.

PAOLA.

Nick? We're going out back!

It's out here. We've got a shed in the garden.

I've soundproofed it with egg-cartons.

For the noise. You know. The neighbours.

RAYMOND.
Tell me about it!

They exit. Pause. Sound of drumming - the kit checked piece by piece. The phone rings PAOLA comes back and answers it.

PAOLA.
Paola Prentice.
Ah. Vivien . . . Yes . . . Eight o'clock? Fine.
Monday. Okay . . . Green and blue . . . Yes, whatever, that's fine for me . . . OK . . . No problem. Monday at eight.
Bye.

The bass drum throbs loudly. PAOLA stands listening for a while. The sound evokes something in her. The drumming finally stops. She goes out back.

SCENE TWO

Later. RAYMOND and PAOLA enter.

PAOLA.
He seems happy with everything. So if that's still alright with you...

RAYMOND.
Fine.

PAOLA.
Excellent!
So what d'you think of the drum kit?
Will it do?

RAYMOND.
Absolutely.
It's still new so it'll need to be played in. Adjusted a bit.
But it'll be fine.

PAOLA.
It wasn't cheap. I mean...
Well, it's his birthday and christmas in one.

Pause. RAYMOND *is watching her.*

RAYMOND.
You don't recognise me, do you?

She remembers.

PAOLA.
Oh! I thought so.

RAYMOND.
Raymond.

PAOLA.
The brother.

RAYMOND.
Half-brother.

PAOLA.
Serge's half-brother.

RAYMOND.
Yes.

PAOLA.
Soon as I saw you.
I knew there was something.
I thought, I'm sure I know him.
But . . .

RAYMOND.
The nose.

PAOLA.
And the light was behind you.
So.
Raymond.

RAYMOND.
Been a long time.

PAOLA.
A long time. Ages.
How's things?

RAYMOND.
Okay. Apart from …

He points to his nose.

RAYMOND.
You?

PAOLA.
Me? I'm fine.
As you can see.

RAYMOND.
You've got children now.

PAOLA.
Two. Nick. Nicholas. He's thirteen. And Christopher. Eleven.

RAYMOND.
It's hard to believe! How long's it been?
The last time we saw each other…
Must've been when you two were still together.

Pause.

RAYMOND.
And here we are. Now your son's started drumming!

PAOLA.
Yes.

RAYMOND.
One of those things he's just been *dying* to do. And you're
like, Drumming? Okay, but you'll learn to do it properly.

PAOLA.
Yes.

RAYMOND.
So you put the ad in the paper.

PAOLA.
Drum teacher required. Yes.

Pause. She starts to backtrack.

PAOLA.

Of course, I'm not sure yet if it's actually going to happen. I mean if it's going to be you. The truth is there's another guy interested.

RAYMOND.

Ah. Right.

PAOLA.

He's a young chap - from the academy actually - he's really keen. To be honest, I've sort of already half-promised him. He phoned me during the week because he thought he might not be able to do it. He's got exams.

That's why I asked you to come round. Just in case. So if he couldn't do it I wouldn't be left in the lurch. You know.

But he said he can. So I have to give him first refusal.

RAYMOND.

Of course.

PAOLA.

He can only do Tuesdays.

Damn. Tuesdays! What did we say?

Tuesdays or Thursdays?

RAYMOND.

Thursdays.

PAOLA.

Och. I completely forgot. He's got computer club on Thursdays. It's the school. They changed it.

I'm sorry, I got it confused. It was put back.

We should've been talking about Tuesdays. Not Thursdays.

RAYMOND.

Tuesdays.

PAOLA.

You can't make Tuesdays can you. It would have to be Wednesday then.

RAYMOND.

Wednesday. I could always rearrange some things.

PAOLA.
  I couldn't ask you to do that. It's too much.
  Damn. It's not going to work, is it. I've brought you out
    here for nothing. I'm sorry.

RAYMOND.
  Don't worry.

PAOLA.
  It's a nuisance though, isn't it?

RAYMOND.
  No. It's good to've seen you again.

PAOLA.
  I'm really sorry. I'm so forgetful these days.

RAYMOND.
  It doesn't matter. It's fine.
  Well.
  I suppose I ll be seeing you.

PAOLA.
  I'll get the door. The handle. It's a bit awkward.

SCENE THREE

RAYMOND *is standing holding a glass of water. Sound of
drumming.* PAOLA *enters wearing her coat. She is
disappointed to have missed the lesson.*

PAOLA.
  Ach! I couldn't get away in time. Some old dear kept me
    cornered for an hour. Gave me her whole life story.
    Then the car wouldn't start.
  Did Nick let you in?

RAYMOND.
  Yeah. We've just finished.

PAOLA.

I wanted to be here. You've actually got him started then?

RAYMOND.

Lesson one. Posture. Holding the sticks. Tightening the
skins. Just the basics.

PAOLA.

How was he?

RAYMOND.

Okay.

PAOLA.

He's doing as he's told, isn't he? I mean, he'd better be.
He can be really difficult sometimes.

RAYMOND.

I didn't have any trouble.

PAOLA.

Don't take any cheek from him. If he starts any of that just
get him told. He needs a tight rein.
I mean, he won't get very far with his attitude.
Drink?

RAYMOND.

I've had some water, thanks.

PAOLA.

Would you like anything else? A beer?

RAYMOND.

No. I can't. Thanks.

PAOLA.

Sit down at least.

They sit down.

PAOLA.

So. Here you are after all!

RAYMOND.

Yes. Your other guy couldn't make it then?

PAOLA.
No.

RAYMOND.
Lucky my Wednesdays were suddenly free, wasn't it.

PAOLA.
Great.
Lessons are really important.
He didn't want them at first -
It was 'What do I need lessons for?'
I just told him -
'Listen pal,
I'm not letting you just fritter away.
If you want to be a drummer,
You're going to learn properly.
No skiving. I've seen enough wasters in my time.
You're not going to be another one!'

I thought about sending him to the Academy. But . . .
You know. That's four years.
And you have to read music.
He's not keen on that. He's done a bit of it before.
Two years of piano. But it was,
'Drumming from sheet music? No way!'

Pause.

RAYMOND.
You haven't seen Serge since…
Since then?

Pause. PAOLA *is defensive.*

PAOLA.
I bumped into him a couple of years ago. In the street.

RAYMOND.
He phoned me last week. He's in Dakar.

PAOLA.
Dakar?

RAYMOND.
Been there a year now.

Pause.

PAOLA.
D'you do a lot of teaching?

RAYMOND.
It's just a sideline. I've got a studio at home. Digital. But I really like working with the kids. It's great watching them realise that there's more to it than just counting to four and bashing things!

I do session work too.

PAOLA.
Oh?

RAYMOND.
Played on a lot of tracks in my time.

PAOLA.
Really? You'll have to let me hear some.

RAYMOND.
Yeah. I'll have a rake through my back catalogue.
Yeah. A session drummer.
It was really difficult for a while.
Lot of people use computers now.
Not everyone though.
Some people still have some sense. Thank God.
They realise it's not the same. Just too … clinical.
They still want proper drummers. Real live ones!

Pause.

Was talking about you the other day. To my mum.
Said she saw yours. Saw her in the street. Few weeks ago.
So she says.

Says she's still looking well. Your mum. Still a bit of a daftie. But she was always a wee bit daft, wasn't she. Getting by on one kidney. She still just got the one kidney?

PAOLA.
Yes.

RAYMOND.

I remember her. In that sweet shop you had. All that
chocolate. And her going on about it. Her kidney.
'Mrs Melt-in-the-mouth' we called her. And you were -

PAOLA.

'Little Miss Melt-in-the-mouth.' I know.

Pause.

RAYMOND.

How long were you with Serge again?

PAOLA.

Nearly two years. If I remember right.

RAYMOND.

Was it that long?

PAOLA.

It must've been. I can't remember exactly. It's been a long
time.

RAYMOND.

Ages.
How old would I have been? Fourteen? God.
That's only a year older than your boy is now.
Serge must've been twenty-one. So you...

PAOLA.

Nineteen. Turning twenty. I think. Yes.

RAYMOND.

Yes.
When I was teaching Nick, I thought –
What if he could see me now?
If Serge could see me teaching Paola's son.
He'd be gobsmacked. My brother. He'd be speechless.

PAOLA.

Yes.

Pause.

RAYMOND.

So you're divorced?

PAOLA.
Yes.

RAYMOND.
Long time?

PAOLA.
About eight years now.

RAYMOND.
Just didn't work out?

PAOLA.
It just got to the point where we'd both had enough.
We were stuck in a rut, I suppose. He was always working.
Sixteen-hour days. Seven days a week.
He was in antiques. Import, export.
From the far east and everything.

RAYMOND.
I'm still living at home. Me and my mum.

PAOLA.
Yes?

RAYMOND.
It suits us both. For now.

PAOLA.
You have plans?

RAYMOND.
Just my drumming. It's all I'm interested in at the moment.
Hah. Look at me. I became a drummer too!

PAOLA.
Like your brother.

RAYMOND.
Yeah.

PAOLA.
I wouldn't have thought of you . . .

RAYMOND.
They made me finish school first. The drumming came later.

Pause.

RAYMOND.
So you really had no idea? When I phoned you about
the ad? That it was me?

PAOLA.
No idea.

RAYMOND.
Me neither. 'Ms Prentice!' To me you were always just
Paola. Crazy Paola!
Raymond Henderson. Didn't ring a bell?

PAOLA.
'Fraid not.

RAYMOND.
Of course. It wouldn't. Serge kept his real dad's name.

Pause.

PAOLA.
It took months before he would even tell me his first name.

RAYMOND.
Serge?

PAOLA.
He didn't want to have a name.

RAYMOND.
What d'you mean?
What did you call him then?

PAOLA.
Nothing. 'He'. 'Him'.

Pause.

RAYMOND.
He went to Burundi for a while.

PAOLA.
Burundi?

RAYMOND.

He was there nearly two years. In the jungle. Miles from
anywhere. Recording tribes. For some record company
in Paris. He was in Morocco too. Spent quite a while
there.

PAOLA.

In the mountains?

RAYMOND.

How did you know?

PAOLA.

There was a time - back then. It was all decided. We were
going to go to Morocco for a year. Visit the drummers
up in the mountains.
The Moroccan mountain drummers.

RAYMOND.

It never happened.

PAOLA.

It was all arranged. We were ready to go. I'd even taken
a year out from college. Then he suddenly changed
his mind.

RAYMOND.

He said it was you who didn't want to go.

PAOLA.

No. It was him. He couldn't give up the group.

RAYMOND.

You wouldn't stand up to the heat. It'd be too much. That's
what he said. You'd never survive in the climate.

PAOLA.

No.

RAYMOND.

I remember.

PAOLA.

You're wrong.

RAYMOND.
I'll ask my mum.
She'll know.

Pause.

It wasn't long after that. The raid.

Pause.

PAOLA.
I don't remember. Not anymore.

RAYMOND.
If you'd gone to Morocco they'd never have caught him.

PAOLA.
No.

RAYMOND.
Two years in prison.
Not much of a holiday.

Pause.

He was always the same.
Always taking things to the extreme.
Always taking chances.
The record deal.
That German tour.
Extremely risky.
Extremely unlucky.

Pause.

That raid.
It was the end.
Wasn't it.

Mum went through hell.
All that time.
Her eldest boy.
All those debts.

And the opportunities!
All the opportunities he had!

What a waster.
Stupid fuck.

A beat.

PAOLA.
I have to get dinner started.
I'm sorry.
You can find your own way out. Can't you?

See you next week.

SCENE FOUR

PAOLA.
It was one of those first nights.
Sweltering hot.
We'd just left a party.
We got stopped.

RAYMOND *nods.*

RAYMOND.
'Where are you off to?'
'Don't know yet.'
'Watch your mouth, prick.'
The usual crap.

PAOLA.
It was all new to me.
I had no idea. Straight out of convent school.
I was shaking like a leaf.
Just like in his room. That first time.

RAYMOND.
Yeah?

PAOLA.
Hang your coat in there, he said.

CHRISTINE 2	You mustn't go to any trouble.
NORA 2	It's no trouble.
CHRISTINE 2	Well, then... thank you. Thank you. If there was a little something for me, I would gladly take it.
NORA 2	Then I'll ask him. You must feel very proud to work. I've never... I've never.
CHRISTINE 2	I like it. It gives me – options. I don't believe money makes you happy, but it certainly does give you options. And it also gives me purpose. Because the truth is sometimes, Nora. Sometimes I feel so... I feel ever so, well, you know.
NORA 2	No. I don't.
CHRISTINE 2	Then you must be very happy. Very proud to keep a home.
NORA 2	You think I am foolish?
CHRISTINE 2	No, never. A woman can do as she wishes. Tell me then, what are you most proud of? Your children?
NORA 2	Yes. I suppose.
CHRISTINE 2	You're uncertain?
NORA 2	No. Well...
CHRISTINE 2	Do I sense a secret?
NORA 2	No, I...
CHRISTINE 2	Tell me! We must always talk the truth to each other.
NORA 2	Well. If we are talking of the truth.
CHRISTINE 2	Always.

NORA 2	You're right. The thing I feel most proud of is – a secret. A secret, that if I am going to share it, you must swear to keep it and not even share it with your shadow.
CHRISTINE 2	I swear.
NORA 2	And she explains that there was a time when her husband was very ill. He lay in bed for months, unable and fading – for reasons that fail her.
NORA 3	Because it was something to do with the pressure of the world changing. He had spent just a few months in France, far enough away from the front line so as to keep all his fingers. But it seems part of him had been damaged because he never did stop jumping at the sound of doors slamming.
NORA 2	The Swinging Sixties seem to have swung in a direction away from him. The traditions he clung on to were crumbling, so he found himself stumbling to find his place in this new landscape.
NORA 1	Because magazines and the TV and the internet and just about everyone he met reminded him of all the things he lacked. Because he didn't own his house or his car and even their furniture was on credit. Which meant there was nothing for him to hold on to when he fell into a state of sadness.
NORA 3	Simply put – he fell apart and so did their finances. And even their savings shrivelled up soon enough.
NORA 1	But they kept on spending and selling the lie that everything was fine.
NORA 2	Because she didn't want her children to worry.

Nothing.
And I'm. I'm panicking.

He's over the wall.
Brains dashed out on a gravestone.
I'm this side.
Out of mind and banging the gate.
But the gate's locked.
There's a dustbin standing there.
So I climb up on that.
But the wall's still too high.
And I keep on trying.
Till I hear this knock.
This knock, knock, knocking
From the other side of the wall.

And I'm 'Is that you?'
Nothing.
So I'm 'Say something damnit!'
Nothing.
Then he's 'Wait. Wait'
'I'll just be a minute!'

Five minutes later. Thump!
He's hopping back over the wall.
Casual as you like.
He'd only battered out a new number!
The knock, knock, knocking was the rhythm he'd found.

RAYMOND.
He was a lunatic back then. Oh yeah.
He could get really manic sometimes.

PAOLA.
Same with the drumming. He was possessed.

RAYMOND.
Drumming's always done that for us.

PAOLA.
For him.

RAYMOND.
Us.

Him and me.
It's in us both.
No choice. Like it chooses you.
My dad - his step-dad.
Hated music. Always did.
'Not under my roof, you don't'
And Serge would snap.
'My dad liked it.'
Serge's dad.

Pause.

RAYMOND.
Serge's dad.

PAOLA.
He played in orchestras.

RAYMOND.
You know?
Yeah. The trumpet.

PAOLA.
Cornet.

RAYMOND.
Yeah?

PAOLA.
It was the cornet.

RAYMOND.
My dad.
Sent him to reform school.
And what a ruckus when he bought his first kit.
My dad snapped the sticks.
Sliced open the skins with a blade.
Threw the thing into the garage.
Slammed a lock on it.
No way.
Serge would never stand for that.
He takes a crowbar. Bingo! Open sesame!

Once he'd started.
Nothing would stop him.

He'd practise in the paint-factory.
In the cellar.
In winter.
Minus ten!

He played with everyone.
They were all rubbish.
Most of the kids had just picked up a guitar.
He was playing with six different groups at one point.
Six of them!

He was hauling that kit about all the time.
And this was before he got a car.
He took it by cart, by train . . .
God, when I started I even used my bike!
Can you believe that?

One time, the roads were all ice.
Perfect!
Swoosh!

The things you do.
Couldn't do it now.
But that was then. It was what you did.
And for what?
Yeah . . .
He was possessed by it. Completely.

A beat.

He nearly drowned once.'Cause of his drums.
Coming back from a gig.
The band in the car.
All the gear in the van.
And the van begins to slide!
Slid right off the road.
Right into a canal.
I wasn't there myself.
I was still too young.
This is just what I heard.
The van.
All the equipment in the back.

And there it was – sinking!
So Serge jumps in to save it.
He was going for his kit.
He'd already had one drum nicked the month before.
No way was he going to lose the rest.

They had to drag him out in the end.
Couldn't swim.
That's the way I heard it.

PAOLA.
That's what he told me. That he nearly drowned.

RAYMOND.
Might've just been a ditch.
Might've grown into a canal.
Over the years.

A beat.

Music.
'You've got to do it your own way.'
'Even if it kills you.'

A beat.

PAOLA.
Taking things to the extreme.
That's just the way he was.

RAYMOND.
Serge was a freak.
But so were you.
Two freaks together!

PAOLA.
Me?

RAYMOND.
Back then? Oh yeah. Absolutely!
The weirdo.
My mum still says that.
That weirdo. The Tart. The Twig.

She never did take to you.
The boys on the street used to call you The Rake.

PAOLA.
I wasn't that skinny.

RAYMOND.
Not according to them.
'Two bubbles in a straw.'
'Skull on a stick.'
That was you.
You were a big hit with those guys. Very popular.
Just never for very long.
Those high boots you wore.

PAOLA.
It was the style.

RAYMOND.
You were a fashion victim.
That hatchet-haircut you had.
And Serge in that stupid suit.
You looked a complete mess.
Dark eyes. White faces. Like pandas!

PAOLA.
That's how it was then.

RAYMOND.
Yeah.
My brother and all his weirdo girlfriends.

You were really a pain sometimes. You know that?
As soon as you arrived somewhere, you'd want to go
    somewhere else.
You were never satisfied.
Never.
Nothing good enough for you.
You'd be off. And he'd be off after you.
It made him miserable. Serge. All that.
And my mum.
'Why does he make things so difficult for himself?'
You weren't the easiest of people.

PAOLA.
> Neither was he!
> The time we lived together. That place down by the carpet
> > factory.

RAYMOND.
> What? The 'cave'? That pit!
> God, that place was tragic.

PAOLA.
> We shouldn't have moved down there.
> But he needed the space for his drums.
>
> My sister tried to put me off.
> 'You'll never be happy with him.'
> 'You'll only live to regret it.'
>
> But we were so wrapped up in each other.
> We couldn't get enough.
>
> We were hooked.

RAYMOND.
> To that shit.

PAOLA.
> Each other.

RAYMOND.
> That shit too.

PAOLA.
> No.

RAYMOND.
> Serge was. The whole group was.
> They really got into it. Big time.
> Should've heard them.
> Like a pharmaceutical convention.
> Just swallowing and snorting.
> God the amount they shovelled up their snouts.
> A truckload!
> They snorted an absolute fortune.
> Snorted and smoked it.

PAOLA.
Serge didn't smoke.

RAYMOND.
Not Serge.
But Frankie. And Patrick.
Like chimneys.
Big fat ones.
Before every gig.
Swallowing. Snorting. Smoking.
Everything!

PAOLA.
Shooting.

RAYMOND.
No.

PAOLA.
Frankie injected.

RAYMOND.
He had diabetes.

PAOLA.
He fed you that old story too?
He was shooting up.

RAYMOND.
He was not!

PAOLA.
You never saw him when he didn't have his works with
    him. He'd have stuck a tent peg into his arm!

RAYMOND.
There's no way he was injecting. I would've known.

PAOLA.
The creases in his arms were all blue.
Blue. Red. And Purple.
His arms looked scary. Full of tattoos.
Daggers with blood. Snakes. Love and Hate.
Frankie. He was hooked on every kind of needle.

RAYMOND.

He was no junkie.

PAOLA.

No junkie ever admits it.
It's broken up enough bands.

RAYMOND.

Not as many as broke up over women.
Women come into play and it's game over.
The complaints start. The whinging about things.
The minute they're married - the band's finished.

PAOLA.

I never came between him and his music.

RAYMOND.

I never said you did. I'm talking about other bands.
Women ruin everything.
You just can't mix the two.
Like working and gigging.
You can't do both!

On top of it all, you've got to rehearse too.

It's a balance. Not many can get it right.
Serge wasn't one of them.
It's even harder for a drummer.
Much tougher than playing a guitar.
Exhausting.
I'd lose three or four pounds every gig. At least.
Eventually you get used to it.
But it's not just the playing.
There's all the other stuff too.
Setting it up. Breaking it down.
You do all that yourself. No-one else can help.
Otherwise you lose things. Bits go missing.

Pause.

PAOLA.

After all that, what chance have you got of being able to
sleep . . .

RAYMOND.
It's hard. Really hard.
But you just have to deal with it.

PAOLA.
. . . All that hanging around for ages afterwards . . .

RAYMOND.
It's not that.

PAOLA.
. . . All the drinking . . .

RAYMOND.
Not that either.

PAOLA.
. . . The wanting to drive . . .

RAYMOND.
The thing about driving is always getting stopped.
A drummer without a driving licence?
That's a disaster!

PAOLA.
As soon as it starts
You know how it's going to end

That everything gets so completely destroyed . . .

We loved each other to bits.

RAYMOND.
Loved? You tore each other to bits!

PAOLA.
No.

RAYMOND.
You had a fling with Fat Pat!

PAOLA.
No.

RAYMOND.
Not a fling then.
But you ended up in bed with him.

PAOLA.
> I don't remember any more.
> Maybe.

RAYMOND.
> Yes!
> I remember.
> You'd dumped Serge.
> Or he'd dumped you.

PAOLA.
> We fell out all the time.

> *Pause.*

RAYMOND.
> I spied on you once. You and him. Did you know that?

> You were at our house. Mum was out.
> You were lying on his bed. I was watching from the attic.
> That crack in the ceiling. Enough to see your legs.
> You didn't know?

PAOLA.
> I said
> Your little brother's spying on us.
> The snotty little rat has gone crawling into the attic
> 'Cause mummy wouldn't buy him new trainers.

> *Pause.*

RAYMOND.
> Anyway.
> You're nothing special to look at.

PAOLA.
> It's time I threw you out.

RAYMOND.
> Yeah. It's late.

> Those boots though. I still remember them.
> God. They were such a turn-on.

SCENE FIVE

PAOLA.
> D'you remember that?
> In Daisy Street?
> The woman who was murdered?

RAYMOND.
> Vaguely.

PAOLA.
> We'd been there a month.
> She lived next door to us. With her husband.
> I'd seen her a few times. In the newsagent.
> With her daughter.
> Must've been three or four.
> Saw them the day before it happened.
>
> Seemed they never argued.
> Never had a fight.
> She was seen drinking that afternoon.
> She was a drinker.
> But no-one had ever seen her drunk.
>
> Sunday evening it was.
> Serge was in his studio. Drumming.
> I was there too. Reading.
> About eight it happened.
>
> She stabbed him with a breadknife.
> Stuck him in the arm.
> He went and fetched his gun.
> Shot her.
>
> First shot.
> The whole street was at the door.
> Tried to break it down.
> There was a second. Then a third.
> Serge was banging out this rhythm he'd been working on.
> The beats and the shots. They must've coincided.
> We never heard a thing.
> The ambulance sirens. That's all. Only then.

And outside everyone was talking about it.
That's how we found out what had happened through the
    wall.

'How could she do something like that?'

RAYMOND.
    Why did she?

PAOLA.
    Serge didn't want to discuss it.
    Didn't want me to even think about it.
    'You shouldn't brood about stuff like this.
    It's not good.'
    Difficult not to think about it though.
    Him. He could just drum it all away.

    Pause.

PAOLA.
    He's starting to pick it up, isn't he?

RAYMOND.
    He's getting there.
    He's keen to learn. You can sense that.
    Much too heavy-handed of course.
    All that youthful raw energy.
    It's always the same in the beginning.
    He has some exercises to do.
    He needs to practise them.
    A lot.
    Every day.
    It's essential.

    Pause.

RAYMOND.
    Serge's group. I've still got tapes of some of their gigs.
    You should hear them now.

PAOLA.
    They were good.

RAYMOND.
    Not really.

PAOLA.
Come off it!

RAYMOND.
Musically?

PAOLA.
They were really tight.

RAYMOND.
Patrick was a rotten bass player.
On the tapes, he's out of tune half the time.

PAOLA.
Patrick. Okay.

RAYMOND.
And Serge.
Some places he can't even hold the beat.

PAOLA.
Yes? Well. I don't know. Musically. I'm not qualified to say.

RAYMOND.
Missing cues. Losing the rhythm. Out of time with each
    other. And the songs!
You should listen to them. God awful some of them.

PAOLA.
Frankie's.

RAYMOND.
No actually. His aren't too bad.
It's the ones they came up with together.
When they were all half-wasted.
The 'difficult' ones.

PAOLA.
Experimental.

RAYMOND.
Shite. That's what it was.
I listen to the tapes and I think,
Christ, what were these guys on?

PAOLA.

Aberdeen. There was a gig that never really took off.
No atmosphere. I remember it clearly.
They just didn't spark that night.
But in Newcastle.
Or that night at the Venue.
Or the Trocadero gig.
Paisley. Liverpool. Manchester.
That whole time.
Everything before . . .

RAYMOND.

Everything before the tour?

PAOLA.

It was amazing. Electric. The energy.
They exploded onto the stage.
Of course you, you weren't there.

RAYMOND.

No.

PAOLA.

The crowd would go crazy.
Every single time.

RAYMOND.

I believe you.
But the tapes.
All I hear is a bunch of guys falling apart.
How they got a record deal - and then a tour - out of it is
    beyond me.
I just don't see it.

PAOLA.

Because they were different.

RAYMOND.

How?

PAOLA.

The line-up. Drums. Bass. Keyboards.
No-one else was doing that.

RAYMOND.
There were loads.

PAOLA.
Later, yes. Not then.

RAYMOND.
Even then.

PAOLA.
No.

RAYMOND.
Do you want me to name them? I could give you a list!

PAOLA.
Not here. Not in England. Not in Europe.

RAYMOND.
It's only my opinion.
I'm just saying.
I listen to those tapes and I don't understand how they got
away with it.

PAOLA.
They worked hard.

RAYMOND.
Them?

PAOLA.
They rehearsed all the time.

RAYMOND.
Rehearsed? They just pissed about.
Frankie could never get everyone together.

PAOLA.
Serge rehearsed a lot.

RAYMOND.
Serge played on his own.
That's just ego-tripping.
Rehearsing's about learning to play together.
You can hear the difference on the tapes.
They never rehearsed as a band!

A beat.

RAYMOND.
  You probably don't know, but you were banned from their
    little den. Forbidden territory.

PAOLA.
  I didn't want to disturb them.

RAYMOND.
  Frankie didn't want you there.
  He couldn't take you pawing at Serge all the time.

PAOLA.
  That's because certain people were jealous.
  He thought Serge should've been his.
  He only had to look in my direction and his lordship would
    start to get uptight.
  And I don't have a problem with gay men.

RAYMOND.
  Frankie wasn't gay.

PAOLA.
  No? He was always trying to touch Serge up. Even while
    I was sitting there. Not that it bothered me. I knew I had
    nothing to worry about. But all that bitchiness.

RAYMOND.
  Frankie was a transvestite but he wasn't gay!

PAOLA.
  Serge should've dropped him right at the start.

RAYMOND.
  Serge was nothing without Frankie.

PAOLA.
  Frankie was nothing without Serge!

  A beat.

RAYMOND.
  You don't know anything about music.
  You've never been in a band like that.
  What would you know?

PAOLA.

I know that they were always fighting.

RAYMOND.

So what?

They would always sort it out.

PAOLA.

They would fall out every day eventually.

RAYMOND.

If they were any good at all it was because of Frankie.

PAOLA.

When he wasn't falling off the stage.

RAYMOND.

And Serge wasn't falling over his drums.

PAOLA.

That only happened one time.

RAYMOND.

Three!

Pause.

PAOLA.

Those moments after the gig, when they'd all been dropped
off, the van taken back, those were the best.

We'd drop into Martha's for a fry-up. He would still have
a few hours before work. So we'd wander through town.
Down along the river.

Summertime. The light gleaming on the warehouses at the
south dock. Him on a bollard. Like behind his drums.
Me on top. Lazy. Feeling good. Between the BP barrels.
Yellow and green.

On that bollard. And it's the first time. Intense. Hold back.
Do nothing. Give nothing.

'How long have we been going?'

'Do other people go on so long?'

His hands on my backside.

'See those oil drums.

The Caribbeans beat them out and play music on them.'

Even then.
Drumming!

One saving grace at least.
The sex was great.

RAYMOND.
Your son. He's not Serge's is he?!

PAOLA.
No.

RAYMOND.
Could have been.
You get couples who fight then go and have a kid to make
up again.

RAYMOND *laughs.*

I might've been an uncle!

A beat.

I asked my mum about this.
She said you had a thing with fat Pat.

PAOLA.
No.

RAYMOND.
Said Serge was devastated.
He followed you.
Found out you'd been cheating.
So she says.

PAOLA.
It wasn't like that.
It was nothing.
When you're that age you get up to allsorts.
You don't know what you're about.
Do anything.
Try anything.

RAYMOND.
Like sleeping around.

PAOLA.

> You don't know anything about love.
>
> You've never been in a relationship like that.
>
> What would you know?

> *A beat.*

RAYMOND.

> I know.
>
> I know that the 'legendary German Tour' never happened.
>
> Hamburg. Frankfurt. Berlin.
>
> All cancelled.
>
> I remember the talk about the great article in Melody
>   Maker. All about how committed they were.
>
> Yeah right.
>
> 'The Band on the Brink of Bigness'?
>
> Bullshit!

> Straight off the ferry.
>
> They're headed for Hamburg.
>
> The van a bit dodgy. As usual.
>
> They're on a different planet.
>
> Stoned out their minds. As usual.
>
> Got completely lost.
>
> Careered off the road.
>
> Smack!
>
> Straight into an electric generator.
>
> The speakers aren't secured. As usual.
>
> So everything's just thrown forward.
>
> Serge cracks two vertebrae.
>
> Frankie loses a tooth.
>
> Patrick's bass is in bits.
>
> They try ringing for a breakdown truck.
>
> No chance.
>
> German tour? Oh yeah.
>
> German language? Forget it!

> Then they go round bragging about their famous gigs in
>   Europe. To everyone. My mum even.

> *A beat.*

PAOLA.

> Your mum never bothered to visit Serge in hospital. When he was laid up with his back. She never came once.

RAYMOND.

> Only because you were there all the time!

PAOLA.

> My son says he's a better drummer than you are!
> He told me yesterday.

RAYMOND.

> Stupid brat! Thinks it's so quick and easy.
> There's more to drumming than just whacking a dustbin with a crowbar!

SCENE SIX

Raymond's studio. RAYMOND is sitting still. The doorbell rings. He rises and answers it. PAOLA enters.

PAOLA.

> Ah.
> I'm here to say that you don't need to come tomorrow.
> My son is being punished.
> He got a letter from school last week. Really bad.
> So.

RAYMOND.

> I was going to phone you anyway.
> I can't make it tomorrow.
> There's a band interested in me.
> I need to call round and see them.
> I know the bass player.
> So it's looking likely.
> So yeah.
> For the next few weeks.
> They've already got a gig. Next month.
> If I'm going to have to learn all the songs . . .
> I'll have to see how it goes.

If I can do both.
Rehearse and teach.

SCENE SEVEN

Raymond's. PAOLA *is at the door.*

PAOLA.
I don't know what to do.
My son. He didn't come home last night.
I don't know who else to ask.
I know he's been hanging around the clubs down by the
    station. You couldn't go and see if he's there, could you?
Would you? For me?

SCENE EIGHT

Paola's. Sound of drumming.

PAOLA.
I don't know for sure. I think I might've reported Serge to
    the police.

RAYMOND.
You reported him?

PAOLA.
I don't think so. I'm not sure.
Maybe.

RAYMOND.
You are crazy!

PAOLA.
If two dogs are stuck together,
Fucking each other,
You throw a bucket of water.

Someone had to separate us.
We were killing each other.
We were dead.
The zombie.
That's what my sister called me.

RAYMOND.
And you turned him in . . . ?!

PAOLA.
To save us both.
Him and me.
Both our lives.
The Zombie.
I was transparent.
My skin was so thin.
I was a nervous wreck.
Couldn't even look at people.
I'd start to whimper.

One night I made a note.
His name. In letters cut from the paper.
And an arrow. 'Drugs.'

They would have to split us up.
They would force us to come off each other.
Cold turkey.
It was the only way.

RAYMOND.
So you sent the note to the cops?

PAOLA.
I put it in an envelope.
Then went out.
I meant to put it in the post-box.
I think I lost it on the way there.

RAYMOND.
You think?!

PAOLA.
I lost it.

RAYMOND.
    Brilliant!
    Same old story.
    Stupid musicians and crazy women!
    Who the fuck does something like that?!

PAOLA.
    I don't think I did it.
    It couldn't have been me.
    It was months later before they actually busted him.

RAYMOND.
    Congratulations. Another classic ending!
    It's like a fucking Johnny Cash song.
    The Ballad of Serge and Crazy Paola!

He walks away then comes back after a while.

    I've been thinking.
    Your son. This has nothing to do with him.
    It's not his fault.
    So, I've decided to keep coming.

PAOLA.
    Don't bother.

RAYMOND.
    I want to.

PAOLA.
    For Nick's sake?
    He told me you can't keep your hands to yourself.

RAYMOND.
    Ha. He's just trying to stir up trouble.

A beat.

    You didn't have to report Serge. They already had their eye
        on him. A long time before your stupid note.
    He was already serving four months suspended.
    And it wasn't even possession they did him for.
    It was the stolen radios. You see?
    He's perfectly capable of fucking things up without your help.

PAOLA.
    Get out of here.

RAYMOND.
   I'm gone.

He remains standing.

PAOLA.
   When I was pregnant
   I'd feel him kicking.
   It used to wake me
   Middle of the night.
   I'd drum my fingers
   On top of my belly.
   I dreamt a few times it was his.
   The kicking had rhythm.

   To hear a rhythm in all things.
   To tap a rhythm into everything.

   We did it all the time.
   Along the canal bank.
   While we were walking.
   I'd do it as well when he was still small.
   Nicky. Nick.
   Out in his pram
   He loved every second.
   We walked every day.
   Two or three hours.
   All over town.

   When he started to walk.
   My husband couldn't stand it.

   All that walking.
   Stopping.
   Falling.
   Getting up.
   Walking further.
   Stopping.
   Falling.
   Getting up.
   Walking further.

   End.

A Nick Hern Book

The Ballad of Crazy Paola first published in Great Britain
in this version as a paperback original in 2001
by Nick Hern Books Limited, 14 Larden Road, London W3 7ST

An earlier translation of this play by Nadine Malfait was
published in 1997 under the title *Drummers* in an anthology
of *Dutch and Flemish Plays* also published by Nick Hern Books

Typeset by Country Setting, Kingsdown, Kent CT14 8ES
Printed and bound in Great Britain by Biddles of Guildford

A CIP catalogue record for this book is available from
the British Library

ISBN 1 85459 667 5